KU-342-982

First published in the UK in 2009 by Bloomsbury Publishing Plc
50 Bedford Square, London WC1B 3DP
www.bloomsbury.com

Bloomsbury is a registered trademark of Bloomsbury Publishing Plc

ISBN 978-1-4081-1508-4

A CIP catalogue record for this book is available at the British Library.

Published in the US by Free Spirit Publishing Inc, 217 Fifth Avenue North, Suite 200, Minneapolis, MN55401-299 Help4kids@freespirit.com

Printed in China by Leo Paper Products

This book is produced using paper that is made from wood grown in well-managed forests. It is natural, renewable and recyclable. The logging and manufacturing processes conform to the environmental regulations of the country of origin.

3 5 7 9 10 8 6 4

Tails Are Not for Pulling

If pets could talk,

what do you think they'd say?

Woof!
Meow?

Squeak
squeak
Chirp!
Glub glub...

But what does that mean?
Maybe...

Fur is for petting.

Backs are for scratching.

Noses are for
nuzzling.

And tails are not
for pulling!

Sometimes pets get scared.

They think you're going to hurt them,

even if you
don't mean to.

Watch and listen closely:
a pet may try to warn you.

BITE!

That's a pet's way of saying, "**Hands off.**"

Pets are for cuddling,
not squeezing.

Pets are for loving,
not teasing.

Purrrrrrr

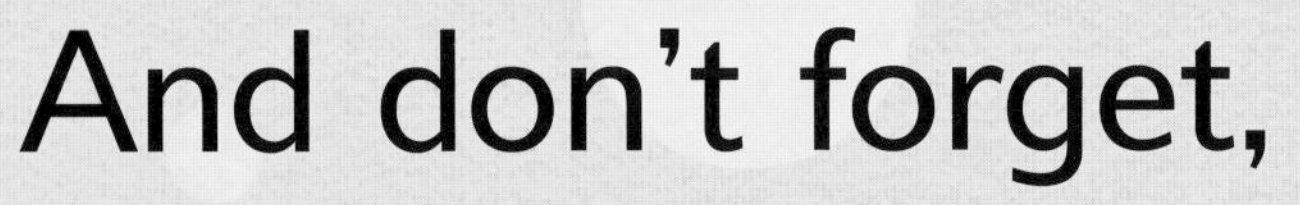
And don’t forget,

tails are not for pulling...

...they're for wagging!
Slurp!

Tips for Parents and Caregivers

Little ones can learn important lessons about treating an animal kindly, especially when given lots of opportunities to observe, feed, handle and play with pets. As you supervise children during these activities, remind them about the importance of treating animals with care. Here are some other 'pet-friendly' tips:

- Use this book interactively. Invite your child to point to the pictures of different pets and give them names. Ask questions as you read: 'Which animals look soft? Which ones have tickly whiskers?' Talk about ways to show kindness to animals: by feeding them, keeping their homes clean, giving them treats and touching them gently.

- Help your child be a friend to animals. Whether you have pets or not, a toddler will probably encounter animals from time to time. Encourage a love for animals by talking about them and reading books that have animal characters. Point out the pets, birds, reptiles or bugs you see each day.

- Show your child how to pet a pet. Young children may express their affection with a bit too much exuberance. They could try to ride the dog's back, pick up the cat and squeeze her, pull the rabbit's ears, or grab the bird from its perch. Show your toddler the right way to pet a pet: slowly, quietly and gently. If more practice is needed, spend time with your child petting stuffed animals. Use the reminder: 'Slowly, quietly, gently', in a soft voice.

- Discourage teasing. Toddlers might try to have fun by taking an animal's toy or bothering a pet while it's sleeping or eating. Even the gentlest pet may bite if a child tries to take away its food or if playtime gets too rough. Gently intervene if your child bothers an animal.

- Teach the warning signs. Animals have ways of telling us to stand back. Help your toddler understand what a pet might be saying when it growls, barks, or hisses. Let your child know that even the sweetest looking pets have sharp claws and teeth.

- Talk about why 'tails are not for pulling'. It can be difficult for toddlers to resist their natural impulse to pull an animal's tail. After all, there the tail is, moving back and forth, so easy to reach out and grab! Explain that it hurts an animal when you pull its tail (and ears, feathers, or fur) or poke its eyes. Remind your child that animals feel pain just like people do, and that they deserve our love and respect.

Staying Safe: Some toddlers are frightened of animals; others may rush in and touch any animal they see. Either way, it's important that children learn how to carefully approach animals, especially ones they don't know. Have a rule to 'ask first'. Before touching a pet, you and your child should ask the owner if it's okay. Teach your child to approach animals slowly. Show how to reach out a hand for the animal to sniff, and how to touch it gently. This lesson is important with pets the child already knows and loves, too. Remind your child to approach the family pet slowly and gently, so it isn't startled. An animal that is frightened is more likely to scratch or bite.